MY BEAUTIFUL
BALLOONING
HEART

Up, up and away
My beautiful, my beautiful balloon

My Beautiful Ballooning Heart

poems by
Janice Silverman Rebibo

Coolidge Corner Publishing

ACKNOWLEDGMENTS

Special thanks for copyediting and much more to Ruti Yonah, for cover concept and encouragement to Gidi Koren, to Michal Rebibo for being there in every sense, to Shimon Rebibo for his lovingcare when it counts, and to poet, Deborah Leipziger, for a crucial archeological assist. My sincere appreciation to Dr. Eli V. Gelfand for his wisdom and my life, and endless love to my dad, Henry H. Silverman, for showing me how to enjoy it. Warm thanks to all my family, friends, colleagues, therapists and teachers, readers and sympathetic listeners on both continents. To Betsy Showstack Young for her art, heart and mind. To Susan S. Wolf for words like sycamore. Always remembering Eve, my mother, whose hands have held mine from the first.

The following poems have appeared in the journals and books cited:
Rebibo, Janice. *Zara Betzion* [A Stranger-woman in Zion]: *Collected Poems 1984-2006*, with a foreword by Amos Levitan, Gvanim, Tel Aviv, Nov. 2007: "Zion By Itself" (1-7); "Four Poems for Old Lovers" (1-4); "I Knew There Was a Story Here" (I-IV); "Certain Sweet Enough People"; "The Unseen Water Below"; "Song for a Pretty High-class Hotel"; "Men with Maps". *Bijou Poetry Review*, June 2010: "As He Waited for the Half and Half". *ARC: 20th Annual Journal of the Israel Association of Writers in English*, Tel Aviv, 2008: "Zion By Itself" (poems 1,4,7: "International Incident"; "How it Went Down"; "May the Words of My Mouth"); "The Unseen Water Below"; "Men with Maps"; "As We Walked Through the Commons"; "Building". *Voices Israel 2011: Poetry from Israel and Abroad*, Vol. 37, Voices Israel Group of Poets in English, Jerusalem, Sept. 2011: "Levitating at Last"; "Sparrows or Starlings". *Voices Israel 2012: Poetry from Israel and Abroad*, Vol. 38, Voices Israel Group of Poets in English, Jerusalem, 2012: "What Lurks Underneath". *Muddy River Poetry Review*, Spring 2012: "My Beautiful Ballooning Heart". *Bagels with the Bards Anthology 2012*: "Capturing Contour Lines". *Soul-Lit*, Spring 2012:"How It Has Always Worked". *Voices Israel Newsletter*, July 2012: "Catching the Mouse". *Voices Israel Newsletter*, February 2013: "One Language One Speech". *Bagels with the Bards Anthology 2013*: "Alternative Drama". *Soul-Lit*, Summer 2013 Featured Poet: "Americana"; "Errata"; "Godless"; "Uncontrollable"; "The Hand of God" and "Certain Sweet Enough People". "Kissing" forthcoming in *The Brookline Tab*. "ROSE AROSE" forthcoming in *Muddy River Poetry Review*.

The poem, "My Beautiful Ballooning Heart" was nominated for a Pushcart Prize.

"Up Up and Away", 1967 Grammy Song of the Year: The 5th Dimension, Words and music by Jimmy L. Webb.

Coolidge Corner Publishing
info@coolidgecornerpublishing.com

TABLE OF CONTENTS

ZION BY ITSELF

Zion by Itself

"Zion by itself is not enough"
Adrienne Rich

1) International Incident

Having studied
the ready-made of life
involving me in all these contradictions
where dialogue is possible,
when the phone rings I am prepared for
an international incident involving a seventeen year old boy
away from home, stranded between flights in the city of my birth.
He is surprised that I speak his father's first language, my second,
and I buy him chicken wings and chips and give him spending money.
Even if we are to be the last Jews on earth
in some imperialists' delight – I do this
"lishmah" – for its own sake
and because my love-affair knows no bounds.

2) Stay

In the street, in the heart of a dream town,
it will be as if we have already lived.
In a street, in the heart of the magic city
we'll enter a corner café.
I'll eat a cheese sandwich.
Will he order coffee and tell me his secrets?
It's a systematic process.
Gradually increase the distance
your lover moves away from you.
Teach yourself that you can
remain calmly
and happily
in one place while he goes to another.
For example, if you're watching television
with your lover by your side and he gets up
for a snack, tell yourself to stay.

3) New Year 5766

It is a new year because an entire love has had
an equinox of warming
on rocks beaming in the solar light
solace
and songs of anguish,
as well as the healthy oak of the region,
hickory and a forest of hemlock to orient us.
The silver birch, the arc of peaks indents
increases
steeply forms the sea and dominates our skyline
for miles around marked with rolling hills,
grassy to the north and to the south submerged
deep in the tropical seas,
meeting of the continents
and corroded
volcanic eruptions of ice,
earthquakes, landslides, thicker forests of fir, small farms
flooded and crowned with colossal masses
of wildflowers.
Still, no integrated structure has emerged
to explain our resource models,
and our action plan, not being in compliance,
notes only what comes to us at dawn.
The witnesses would signal to the court in the morning
before all of our burning afternoon offerings,
the singing of the Levites derived from a respect
for the equinox, perhaps,
in the seventh month of the calendar year.

4) How It Went Down

When I was a sweet young thing
I sang the blues
I was a torch singer
They found me dead, no I was
only unconscious or short of breath
surrounded by swiveling office chairs
years later.
I was light as a feather. He lifted
me up and sat me on the kitchen counter
formica
white
The dinner was perfection.
A singer named Barry sliced
the roast
I needed help back then.
Artis had shot a moose and marinated it
in my Corelle serving pieces.
The air was full of sulphur.
Talk about yellow fog!

5) Sticking to the Topic

For those who want to delve more deeply
here is a text that flows with wisdom
and tantalizing unsolved problems because we
do have a theology
and this is its translation.
Though nothing may fully address
your need
to dissect this game, perhaps he
will read the poem straight through
and develop a winning strategy.
I hope
he'll find that even my scholarly summary
is filled with fresh ideas
and one person puzzles with facets like Rubik's Cube.
Those others are trivial games for
two players
and always move to a state where one
can't move.

6) Our Sages Say

He believes we have time
for a final redaction
and in paradoxical fashion
he may be right
though so much work remains to be done and
there is no place to do it.
Our sages say we merely formulate
what came before. No first fruits
for us
whether we reap our sheaves by day
or the whole night through.

7) May the Words of My Mouth

Words of weight and measure
and a lover beyond ten fingers –
no common scale for all.
I want to calculate my grip,
our puzzled pasts by means of
measuring spoons and cups
and paragraphs and pithy sayings and careful
deliberations – precise dimensions for –
nowhere. I sit at home in my homeland and
abroad back home and guesstimate
how to grasp.
Who will clutch at the words of my mouth?
as my spirit expands and contracts
and forms his dust into letters of an alphabet or two.

Four Poems for Old Lovers

1) Oh My Goodness There's an Old Lover

Oh my goodness! There's an old lover
sitting under the trees
on those folding chairs I hate
at the Silky Way Café.
You know, the wooden ones with slats
that might collapse or at least tip over
ungracefully on the gravel
around the round tables
that aren't too stable. Will I say hello?
Sit down and have "a coffee"
in the local lingo. It's been a while.
Smile. The shadows under these trees
were always gentle. Temperamental
was the word I jotted down before
and Tenderly, by chance. His eyes.

2) Death Bed I Love You

I was so intent on letting you off the hook
That I pictured you on your
      deathbed sending me
        that text message.
Or at least following infarction
I love u
And in order to allay my fears
  delete my sadness
I had to plunk you back
   mid-picnic in some god-forsaken
     meadow by a stream
a clearing in the northern woods perhaps
  surrounded by your family and friends
just like last August?
for a week
with no Internet
and very poor cell phone reception.
(Auntie Bess' doctors are on vacation too.)
 You went behind a tree to pee
  and texted me I love you.

3) Lunch with the Last One

When you stroked my arm
on the second floor of that big restaurant
it made me so angry.
We have a history
of good sex
of which I would rather not be reminded.
I am busy making a doormat of myself
right now
with another lover, also flawed, but not bad either.
You'll have to let me alone
to let this run its course
and by the time I've ruined
this one too
by turning into mush
like that bagel-toast we split – too much cheese
we'll all be old
and even Viagra won't help.

4) 3 Floors Up

In the end
court approval came through
to register my old apartment
in the name of a minor child.
It will be sold.
And this within 48 hours
of the death of my darling lover
of years ago. How I waited
for him on that porch
peeking through the shutters
3 floors up
how I waved the shutters
goodbye.

I Knew There Was a Story Here

I

I turned, one foot still on the footstool, my ankles elevated for health and comfort. It was Esther who came in, holding out her hand to receive the envelope.
"Good morning, neighbor," smiled Esther; "am I disturbing you? Just wanted to take my papers."
I nodded my head slightly.
"Just a minute," I replied.
Esther stood there
Her eyes fell on my left ankle, deep red and swollen as never before.
It was late in the morning. I put aside my notebook and straightened up.
"The fax went through."
"Thank you so much."
To be honest, I was concealing from her
The true story behind my apparently innocent
Reclining posture.
It was like all the times I'd lied about my daily doings
Giving the impression that I was working hard in a concentrated
Orderly manner. My bulging veins
Justified the position I liked best. What did it
Matter what I did or did not do. No way to hurry
This. It would be clinched
Whether or not I sat up straight and worked, and
Although it would be better, I thought,
for all concerned
to write about a more significant subject,
this swollen ankle does the trick.

II

Until now, the receptionist
had kept her gaze on the plasma screen.
Steady virtual infirmities marched
across its surface. In the uncertainty that surrounded us,
she would be relying almost totally on the display.

These 3D colored letters
were transmitted continuously because
without them, dissatisfaction could wipe out
entire segments of the teeming complex around us.

As I neared the display, Ms. Purdie's calm face
glanced aside from the plasma screen. "Some of the malcontents
may try to escape. Some are afraid,
I mean." She glanced beyond me then.
"Watch out for those –
the Almost Gone, they're called."

"Okay, great," I said. I knew there was a story here.

III

One night as I was lying with my lover,
I said, "My love, if you love me,
turn on the light
and I will write down this poem
that just came into my head."
My sturdy lover got up, turned on the light
and brought me my pen and notebook. I wrote,
and my lover said, "O mistress of my soul,
won't you read to me what you have written?"
Whereupon I read, "In the hall I think I hear
a heavy man with rubber boots."

IV

"No, it does not!" I said, fiercely. "I do understand!
Don't I? I'm just right for you, and in the end
you will bless the day you first set eyes on me.
I suppose I should hold my tongue. If I do choose to leave
you'll tell everything to that woman,
your wife, and you'll wish to goodness
you'd never caught my eye. I tell you I just won't stand for this.
No one would who knew what I know about you!"

Certain Sweet Enough People

My love, you know that certain sweet enough people bring joy to my life.
Although we may not live in your Uncle Karl's condition
of radical equality, I turn on the TV and there they are,
those friends the singers in upscale flowing dresses, the guys in tee-shirts red and black.
Joy. Our art's a discredit to all that's high, and it's breakfast food human, and public as
popsicles. Those four are my super-sized portion of social wealth, which I squander
with near orgasmic exuberance, I swear. When I too hear strangeness calling I nod obliquely
and stop short of queer. How dull that my best holiday will not be Yom Kippur,
but just some wine and soda Jewish New Year's e-mail to those four just sweet enough
to bring me joy. Who knew before I googled it that strangeness is a quantum number useful for
describing short-lived love. But here I look ahead with such naïve atomic energy and hope.
After all, my love, it is you who may well ask, conjuring up your proud relation, Uncle Karl,
Just how much inequality can this gal tolerate? Especially now, when we've discovered that
certain particles are pre-existing pairs. (O just which particles, I plug away and grin and ask
mid quarky dance, might you and Uncle Karl share? Please show me one day soon!)
Such a strong interaction we've been in my long strange life.

The Unseen Water Below

Because the ground below is soaked with invigorating juice,
I spend hours in the sun digging holes to China.
On our cosmic beach in one-piece suits next to the water,
Betsy and I splash our feet to this day
and the hole fills up faster than we can dredge with our fingers,
our cupped hands, again and again. Intoxicating beverage, salt-free,
or nearly. Scandinavians would have it that our testicles are at risk,
while Canadians assess the dose of soma sacraments or inorganic solvents
and wait for the glaciers' revenge.
When the only way to know what's in a cloudy mixture is to drink it,
cyanide and protozoans, billion year old comet dust,
my father swigs it from a plastic supermarket jug in Boston,
but reconstitutes his minestrone straight from the tap.
Here in the middle east, next to the desert,
it's appealing to think, as Betsy skyped,
that his improved behavior must be due to "something in the local water"
and to pour mine out of the electric kettle into a 6 oz. glass
and hold it up to the light before I drink what's seeped up
from dozens of thousands of meters deep.

Song for a Pretty High-class Hotel

If I have to throw in the towel,
I'm going to do it at the Delta
But first they'll check my credit card,
Which might be a problem.
When we lie down at noon
Down at the Delta
On a web of lies
It's not so bad.
Colleagues and spouses
Can wait in the lobby –
An outstanding buffet
Will satisfy all.
Registration and Breakfast
Introductory Remarks
Keynote Lecture and Workshop
On Ethical Issues,
Down at the Delta
The pillows are downy –
Poor love does his best
Juggling snuggling us all.

Men with Maps

My life is ruled
By men with maps.
They have no choice.
Do I?

Life forms are sparse
In this part of the world
At least those I can see
With my naked eye.

Once I lived next to a frozen river.
The only way I knew that it was safe
was that the logging trucks
had not yet fallen through.

Linda says it is the others
who scare you
not me. Isn't this true?

How do I know when
I've crossed the border?
These twin cats are not a compass,
and this laptop gives up nothing.

Will you go on looking
with your map
at sunset
after the sky has sealed its regrets?

In every apartment in this tenement
a soldier's on WiFi with someone
or listens to Russian music
or strums his guitar.

I try to believe in your gentle touch
but maybe it was only the edge
of an ancient map brushing
my nipples time and again.

Beloved Wife of

The only way to survive this
is to be buried in a foreign language
After a brief illness

Beloved wife of the late
Not even that
and yet
after a spate of dear devoted communications
we could be formerly of here
Longtime residents of some half-moon bay

They have entered into rest
beloved former wife
of the late
and
formerly beloved
husband of the living

"Springtime Mantleth Every Bough"

Let us call her Springtime
like a lilting canzonetta
for three voices
by T. Morley
although she looks like a cold hearted she-dog
beware
in her photo.
Springtime because she is a festival of our freedom
from bondage
to your one extramarital love.
No longer will I dream of winter
by a cozy fire
under the blankets with you
when you're widowed
heaven forbid
for Springtime has come
again
for you.

Ancient Handicraft

Cheaters are liars, of course I knew,
but this latest layer feels particularly sticky.
My times with him, the days and months,
my crazed sense of ethics lightly plastered over
with fascinating flesh and such crafty minds!
With creativity and skill a plasterer can spread it
thick and smooth
and swirl it while it's fresh
for an ornamented finish.
To augment me
not replace,
the professionals would say,
"a dirty job"
soiling shoes and clothing
and physically demanding
standing, bending, lifting,
reaching overhead.
And that topcoat sets so quickly!
Hot on the trail of my lover's trusty trowel
I played my part sub rosa in his wet indiscretion.

As We Walked Through the Commons

As we walked through the Commons early in the morning
I saw what remained of our global love
down on its luck
under US army blankets curled up on the gratings
stretched out on park benches
with a dead rat to grace our path.
Years had passed since I'd walked there
and taken a good look
although I hadn't yet been cast
as America the beautiful who'd lost her crown
as we rushed back to the Harborside Inn
to pack our little bags and say goodbye.

Smoking

He said it happened to him because
he quit smoking.
Well, I'd consider taking up smoking
but one of my husbands died from it
so I won't recommend it to him either.

Do you think that smoking was the secret?
I haven't stopped eating, for example
So what could it be
and I still have my hair (more or less)

"Something in the local water" perhaps?
or the fact that there is no "local" in the water
for me anymore…
zilch.

I said to him
Maybe if YOU wrote, I would.
but that's blackmail, I suppose

and believe me
I know it's all a matter of perspective and that there are
one or two other things going on in this world
besides poetry
love
and a fine cigarette.

Building

I am going to tell you
If I were tied up in places you would untie them
and me. It is I who will tell you
I will be vivacious and fascinating
the real me, like in the movies.
Whenever I am busy erecting alters
I will be the one who is telling you
I can depend on you to tear them down
I am erecting alters to romantic places where we loved
The stone markers I put up every day to witness
our presence, my existence
You will tear them down
I am telling you one by one
just by stepping there with one foot
with both, together with other lovers
until there is no ground on earth for an alter of mine.
Then I will just be me
We will meet in the air I am telling you
When there is no place left to stand.

America Is Plenty

Uncontained

It is often a different picture. Walking
through my gut unlike anything I wish to know.
Have you seen it yet?

Once, when I was not hoping for anything
unfamiliar, the scene came front and center full of
the old river and the logging trucks. How we
treaded the living ice at midnight. How I painted
their yellow furniture white with electric indigo
fleurs de lis.

Then out of my body I went, hardly
contained by the hallway walls, down the stairs to
Martin, who sat at the kitchen table, beyond the
living room, looking the other way.

I stopped short and then, as if spring-loaded,
flew back to the white and blue bed with my head
hanging over the edge.

Beggar Woman of Brookline

Being out on the street today, I ate a half a chicken and ducked into a movie about life and a death thirty years ago. There are so many movies now about back then, and about a little further back, too.

I always wonder whether I was aware of the news at the time. Did I watch it on TV. Where did I live? When I try to straighten out the days of my life I get hungry.

I Watched in Awe

I was wondering whether his name was
John. When I read that Neil Armstrong stepped on
the moon in July, I pictured this John without a
shirt, tall and lean and muscular. Very white. Fair.

He may have been John, or Bob. John may
have been the fellow who helped renovate my house
in Nantasket by the bay, after the storm, with my
second husband. Tall. Muscular. Fair. Without a
shirt, hammering studs in the basement.

That first possible John slept in the back
room for a while, the maid's room, which was our
den with the TV in the big old apartment on
Princess Street, Saint John, NB, in those
draftdodger days. I stood in the kitchen looking
past him at the screen as Armstrong took his first
small step.

There was also a John, a strawberry blonde,
at the apartment complex in Chestnut Hill – on the
gray shirted maintenance staff with Abe when our
kids were little. Definitely John.

Who Cared

We certainly were against the war. I remember the article with the President's caricature in one or the other of those two glossy weeklies – before we left the country, I think. We passed it back and forth. I carried it around U. Mass. and read certain parts again to myself and with Rob, whose graduate deferment was about to end.

It wasn't that I wasn't involved. It is that my memory for names and dates was never any good.

There was the unheated bathroom off the kitchen "up north" – the enclosed end of the front porch – and an oil stove moaning, almost roaring through the nights.

What Lurks Underneath

I have always been obsessed with the way we use language to mask primal urges. No, that is what Boston Globe correspondent, Ed Siegel, quotes about Pinter from Mr. Billington's book in his obituary spread, *Harold Pinter, dramatist of life's menace, dies*, on the day after Christmas 2008.

As the years went by, according to Siegel, Pinter became increasingly interested in political issues. Mr. Pinter called Mr. Blair "'a mass murderer'" over the war in Iraq," writes Mr. Siegel, who builds to the conclusion of his piece by citing biographer "Mr. Billington" (with contributions by Globe staffer Mr. Valencia and wire service material), on Pinter, whose later plays "counterpoint the smokescreen of language."

Americana

When the Red Sox won the Pennant on
October 1, 1967, it had something to do with
spirituality. An eagle, or a feather, no doubt. Rob
entered my realm of possibility, his off-campus
studio filled with significant books. His classical
and jazz collection would nourish countless souls
for countless days. Countless euphoric kids
stomping on the hood of his black Mercury inching
through the square. Souls like rolls of toilet paper
suspended in the air for a moment that night before
they unwound down 22-story dormitory towers,
piling up on the plaza.

Ten Years Before Disco

At seventeen and eighteen, it wasn't easy to
be wise. I can report that there were those who did a
fine job nonetheless. Striped bellbottoms and a
navy blue shirt were a good choice, for example, for
my expatriate photo with backlit spun gold hair on
Terry and Joan's Saint John fire escape. During
visits to Sue and Clark's farm, one young woman,
whose name I don't remember, rarely talked. Her
baked whole apple dumplings with real pie dough
were manna to the group. There, it was Sue, well
over thirty, who declaimed the platform in extreme
and provided shelter to friends, evaders and even
deserters. Or maybe deserters were frowned on
there? Rob, who was twenty-two or twenty-three,
knew the score.

In Memoriam

Stripped to the waist, tanned creamy black,
riding a bicycle on the kibbutz with two lengths of
pipe under his arm, smiling.

Careers

I ran into Stephanie at Brookline Open Studios. Hadn't seen her in over thirty years. A wave of affection. "Stephanie?" I asked in disbelief. In the interim I'd raised two kids and been abroad for twenty years. She was still a community activist, but retired from the Boston Public Schools, where we'd first met in 1974 when court-ordered busing had just begun. She manned the bus stops with all the Teachers in Charge from our seven linguistic communities while I shoved quintuplicate carbon copies into my pocketbook to camouflage my fledgling typing skills.

The Guilty Party

Am I a better person than everyone else in the world because I did not fully formulate the sociopolitical basis for my actions (or did I)? Simple and godlike.

Was my witnessing passive, my participation inadvertent? Or worse: Perhaps my agenda was playful or melodramatic. What's a girl to do!

And this pseudo analysis in retrospect? Are my motivations literary? Psychological? Hormonal? Will the guilty party please stand up.

A consistent longing has not ceased to attach me before I can turn around, again and again. Quickly, I try quickly to assess before I'm swept away.

Safety

When I worked in the vineyards early in the
morning in the spring of 1971, in the Jordan Valley,
they told me that the booms, *haboomim*, were on
the other side – between "them". How close was it?
Like from here to Fenway Park? Out of the corner
of your eye, even an airplane may look like an eagle
flying by. Was I safe?

What is my margin of safety at any given
moment? And much later, farther south: In an
improvised "sealed room" – the kitchen of all places
– the safest I could muster – with two children in
gasmasks in a home with a porous roof? Did I plug
the hole around the kitchen pipes well enough? I
heard the codeword – *nachash tzef'a* – viper (for the
"serpents" that were shot through the skies every
night), woke the children, and we hurried to the
kitchen but couldn't catch the cat. Was that wide,
clear adhesive equivalent to duct tape? Was the
towel under the door wet enough to stop the
venom? Were we safe?

And much later, estranged, far away from
offeret yetzukah – Operation Cast Lead, I am safe. I
am safe here in Brookline, Massachusetts, from the
rain of missile shells bursting full of nails.
Protected from events by a lead apron of distance
that presses on my heart, I keep looking both ways
when I cross the street – left, right and left again –
and buckling up for safety, always buckling up.

Day 16 of Operation Cast Lead

There are wars that never end. They are like
a woman scorned who wasn't too sane to begin
with. Awful things get said. Defamation of
character, to put it mildly. Bloody murder. And
there's no end to it. And whatever you say, she's
smarter and sharper and quicker and can go on and
on without stopping for breath. And she'll give you
herpes on purpose and vandalize your Wikipedia
and drink a jug of wine at night with her downers
and sleep like a baby for a few hours and then be up
at noon to do it all again. She'll use false names
and falser pretenses – anything to keep your balls in
the air. You'll have nothing left but your good will
your good intentions your good deeds and maybe
your wife and children and grandchildren under
your vine and fig tree living in peace and unafraid,
unlike you who vomits every time you read the
headlines in the morning paper or on line.

Errata

Only what is utterly stable is real. Only
what is downright durable is genuine. Only what is
absolutely tough is true. Only what is totally rough
is right. Only what is enormously uneven can be
dead on. Only what is utterly, downright,
absolutely, totally, enormously erratic.

Day 20 – Gloves Off!

Take off the gloves. It's all in how you conduct yourself. And remember, the context is not there for everyone to see. Why not say it out loud: "The kid gloves of disengagement are off." and "If such weapons were loosed on you, wouldn't you take the gloves off?"

Perhaps an iron fist in a hopeful velvet glove for engaging moderation might constitute a calculated risk? All gloves are off.

During the lull, before it was deliberately shattered, was there anyone who advocated "handling with kid gloves"? Who, me? There was so much shuttle diplomacy, I thought I'd never have a place to hang my hat. Gloves off.

Taking the gloves off, let's create significant damage. Hands off. Hands Off. Hands off? Gloves off! Whenever I act humanely, I become a human target – a sitting duck of a woman in the winter of her life. It's all stages and phases from here.

Nevertheless, I will warn you about my offensive in a rain of leaflets and 300,000 phonecalls a day and wait for the all clear before I launch. Although my hit will be direct and explosive, you'll be left untouched, I swear, and the secondary explosion will expose you and your capability to blast me to bits.

In this autobiographical construct that unconscionably manipulates metaphors of war, you'll storm my humanitarian corridor (that flows with milk and honey, a thousand trucks and two score ambulances) firing round after round and waving your white flag. Your hospital bed awaits you. Day 21 is next.

Ongoing Resistance

Soon after that, the comments began flowing in surges. Twenty-three days, and still no end in sight. The muzak played on; the silk suits slid from the stage to the head table. Wherever you looked there were people eating, leaning over their plates, chewing, reaching across the table for more. While all may be well on this home front, in that other place of mine... They were like fat cats that had rushed to their dishes again this afternoon, before any other cat could – what? ...unilateral ceasefire means more rockets. Just enough to keep up the angst. Yes, what joy to be with people who are all busy at their own plates, to eat undisturbed, lick, chew without interruption. All is well on my home front, did I say?

This Day Is Not Numbered

You can go ahead and minimize the print version window – this day is not numbered. My hands were shaking, but I got hold of myself again. They've stopped numbering the days of this war. Although I had counted twenty-three, they are now calling it a "twenty-two day offensive".

I am able to look at myself in the mirror. Here I am, leaning on the sink, talking to myself and at the same time inspecting my new hairdo, ready for the day. That last volatile day, the first of the ceasefire, has been wiped off the books. It struck me, as I closed the bathroom door, how small I'd looked against the expanse of white tile. Now the accounting will be of rubble and ruins, building estimates and projected numbers of weapons to be manufactured or smuggled in. We're all winners, the headlines said. Victorious.

The experts have begun to arrive. The body count is etched in their memories along with the pictures of children in pain. Their hearts have been wrenched with such spasms that they could not help but cry out. By now, holes in living room walls and the group of centenarians spared from death because they'd just gone down to breakfast have become archival footage.

How old I suddenly felt to be still coming all that long way and back again. Just like me, though. Archival footage. Just like Janice. I have the conviction of a... And now the garage door had opened; it had made way for me to embark on this day.

Godless

    "I have no religion now," said Chekhov.
Had he been a poet, would he have had even less?
Wasn't there something in the LA Times about
that? About Roethke and poetry's religious art
being about as godless as you can get? His
unforgettable, inexorable – Oh I've known offices
aplenty, mystical pencils and all.

Not Taking a Stand

    A dear poet who never took a stand
once accused me in print of not taking a stand
in the poem that opened my second collection.
    He seemed to like the poem well enough,
although not as much as the one with all the
references to blackness.
    It had been on just such a dark night on the
cusp of the new millennium that I'd had a dream
about a man, a derelict, lounging against a picket
fence. In my dream, he said something portentous
to me.

They Never Told Me Katherine Mansfield Was Dead

It had been a week like other weeks in this house. Nothing memorable had happened. John hadn't come back from his trip until Friday morning. Where had he been? What had he been doing? He wasn't going to give us any details. Our John, marginalized, slouched over the dining room table and with little interest spoke into the cordless phone as though he dozed: "How long after one dies may one pick up the death certificate?" There was no doubt about it, he was exhausted; he had lost all sense of himself. I tried not to laugh. Even I was not going to be able to reach him this morning. "Who died," I asked. "Who was it?" Round the dining room table, with its flowered linen-like plastic cloth, the figures gathered. Eyes fixed on me, blinked in succession, in syncopated rhythm. The phone was put to rest, the tablecloth smoothed with one hand; eyes were shut to await the words, quietly tensing. "No one you know." Somewhere, around the edge of his present truth, he saw them file out of the room. John rose, as if he just happened to be on his way to the door, saying goodbye to our guests.

America Is Not Enough

America is not enough. Should single mothers go to India to put their kids through college in Seattle, to help their over thirty offspring who surely will contribute to global mental health? I am afraid, dear heart, that the pay's too low even with the headset thrown in.

I have landed. I am in America, totally involved, and America is not enough. Totally self-involved in America, which by itself is not enough, either. Analysts predict that there will be yet another round of layoffs in…

"Overt acts. Talk does not a conspiracy make. He did not do an overt act. He tipped them off to do something, but not necessarily to kill him. Maybe to frighten him. Not that I have any admiration for the guy. There's a legal principle involved here. Just 'cause I tell somebody that I'd like the guy to get beaten up, does that make me responsible for the guy getting beaten up?"

"Maybe there was evidence that she… There you are. There you are."

Plain talk. That is the American way, and it's good enough for me. A little plain speaking. We accept plain English here. Cash only. Keep your laundry lists short and to the point. America is plenty.

Torch Song for Jerusalem

And yet someone needs to be a watchman
on the walls who will not hold her peace, a watch
woman unto the house of Israel. My hireling days
are those of a custodian, ubiquitous in self-imposed
exile. When evening comes, my well-heeled feet
retain no memories of that land except for the
occasional stumble on its pebbles over the course of
twenty-odd years. I have had my mantle lifted from
my shoulders by keepers of her walls by night, my
veil removed.

Rhythm of a Line

What's around the next corner? At last, a statement for the rest of time? Will the rhythm of the next sentence drag us down like sinkers on a fishing line, cast to land our quarry, or ascend in concrete arches to span a surging interval between us? "Proceed," he'll say; "spit it out," when at last my fear subsides. Once spit, the words will take their destined places, grounded, as it were, like cobblestones that still encrust the streets of Beacon Hill – less virtual, more cogent, he'll imply. "What about the hours," I'll finally ask, depressed; "What about the hours, the zones, the world clock of our fantasies in fives now, soon in sevens?" "There's little I can do," he'll then reply.

The Scent of Gehenom

Have you pressed the soles of your feet on cool concrete terrazzo tile in the Judean Desert in September? An erotic dance worth doing, which is the essence of our learning. How starkly a sense is revealed when you cross a line! His Citroen BX once brought a leftist love to me almost against his will.

At the level of language on well-baked Saturdays in 1987, my young family awoke to the scent of burning tires from Coca Cola Junction and knew the word for where we were. As my father's Yiddish saying goes, "What was on the lung was on the tongue," across the green line.

There came no subsequent sweet smell of absolution at the sight of ourselves for the very first time. Oddly, the real estate values had exactly doubled when we sold and split the profits half and half.

Intensity and Frequency

We used to have a soft spot for the force of repetition, and of course for repetition, itself. For some, it seemed to spring from that obstinate *Bolero*, while for others it evolved from pure love of mass production. As for me, being a product of pop culture replication, I would say that, while I never wrote a line on Lana Turner, Jimi Hendrix changed my life at least twice. Matching such pathos underscored my perception of the fundamental nature of mankind – how even at the height of an extraordinary passion there was order and precision far beyond expectation that simply begged imitation. How, even if the experience itself was slightly maudlin, its reproducibility was a basic force of nature and, ostensibly, embodied a fundamental sign of the times. There are days, even now, a millennium away, when I dream of simulating the leaps I took with Jimi, and days when – I swear – I almost do.

Sparrows and Starlings

Sparrows and Starlings (A Love Poem)

House invaders, they will take you over,
inhabit your spaces like a lover in your pores
even the day after the doormen whistled him down
a taxi to the nearby airport. No huge public embrace
before you watched the taxi head for the corner
and you headed for the crosswalk, for the station
right across the street. Charles Street. He had
nuzzled you on the sidewalk and was nervous
that the cabs were not responding to the
whistles, mechanical and strictly human lips
and fingers. And he is in your fingers now, and
hands, while you watch, chin in hand, the sparrows
or starlings through the window to the right of your cherry table
as they flit from the rain soaked wall down to the emerald grass.

Never or Never

Voyage to a university town in late
December with painterly repercussions
in a poem that substitutes
for blossoming.
Never.
Or never will cease to be a desert
visible from every direction, searing,
since you care so, since you care,
ripping out handfuls of frozen grass.

Ducks or Geese (A Done Deal)

I actually saw the ducks (probably geese) flying south
in formation, although it was more or less a straight line.
No going back, I thought. East is to my left down Beacon Street
to Kenmore Square and from there to the Harbor and west is
down Commonwealth more or less to my right, to Newton,
Waltham and beyond, so it is south. South for the winter. I had heard
so many syncopated bird sounds from beyond the yard as I walked
to our door, or from over the fence towards the stone church turned
condo, but no birds there that I could see, and then it registered that this
flurry of voices was quacks (honks? no, must have been ducks),
and I quick looked overhead and turned around and caught them
exiting the north, so high above our half a tree's worth of bright
yellow leaves, all that's left now – lower half only, and the now
golden willows and dayglow green grass, still. They were leaving me
here, exactly here – behind. The contract's signed.

Barbara and the Lemon Tree

One parting look from the broad archway back into the sunken Rhode Island living room, seeing my grandmother happily in "Cousin Barbara", on the wide sofa backlit by vaulted windows. Barbara's dad, the doctor, my great uncle born in Russia died in Delray Beach, had just passed away at 103, ten years after his older sister, my "Ma". My eyes wiped away this cordial cousin and four decades since I last remember seeing her, transformed her into my Ma's smile and motioning, poised, long straight fingers, Ma's knuckles visible from across the room. The crook of her wrist, inverse angle of her index finger, her fingernail as it swept down through the air in the light from the vaulted windows, in profile, was Ma on a webbed beach chair in front of her trailer in San Diego pointing to her lemon tree, or in her Boston knit shop, or cleaning fish at Hymie's before and after they moved out to LA, playing poker and winning, and joyfully holding court in every living room.

Levitating at Last

for Lorisus

Sometimes I think about swallowing swords and instead
decide to become a fire eater. This morning's Herald
has a picture of the lady from Methuen who spied
Jesus on the bottom of her iron. My photo with flaming
mouth belongs beside hers with the flat of her iron
facing the camera, only to me it looks more like the
Mona Lisa. It's all a question of cultural orientation
they say. Once my boss in Israel gave us ironing boards
for Passover. Although I knew I'd had an iron when I moved
to that country years before, God only knows where it went.

Elusive, Oscillating Figure

The overall concert experience took me over as the orchestra bonded with the biography of the composer. It was the symphony orchestra, nothing less than sensational, and that same score, which always made it particularly worthwhile to take him on. That same score from one of the most productive periods of his life. The only new element was the next city to be chosen as he became something more like the financially independent artist he needed to be and wonderfully lyrical. As he liked to put it, he feared the "milieu had been nazified". Understandably, therefore, it helped him personally to open with a rhythmically elusive, oscillating figure – like a chant". Magnificent. You were his youngest assistant then, and there was occasion for a display of sexual energy. Instead, however, he received an imposition of rules, copiously elucidated by you. "Who cared?" he would later say. He had already pondered the problem for a year. Lacking heroes, he had clarified his own ideas enough, boiled his propositions down. Nothing matters so much to a young composer as that initial second of the success of the work, tonight's performance being perhaps the most remarkable of those this writer has experienced with an insider's view of his life, thrust out from the darkness by a new production.

The Author at Sixes and Sevens

Then into the light, which persisted above, and into
                    the calm and the air,
There ambled an author straight from her desk, disheveled,
                    and ready to dare.
She talked like a woman afloat on a lake with hardly
                    a pause or a cough,
Though she dusted the hem of her skirt with her hand, and she took
                    her bed jacket off.
There was one who saw his neighbor's form, but he racked
                    his brain for her name;
And he called his wife, who was first to cheer
                    the author as out she came.

As He Waited for the Half and Half

His meter was not running out
this time, he laughed, and to my left
a white-shirted fellow under forty told his
cropped silver haired woman companion
on the neighboring stool by the window about
"our children's passion" at the Village Starbucks
on New Year's day 2010.

Videoclip in Yellow, Green and Pink

for Betsy

Still sweet, still pretty although I'm not allowed
to photograph today. Only bare branches
and the forsythia yellow behind you
and green grass snatched from the jaws of death.
No chance to improve my angle
because the chairs are welded to the table
that has dried pink juice streaked across it
with a sunshine yellow straw stuck there.
I keep my elbow off the table, my eyes on you
in your paler yellow cotton hat with the curled
brim angled up higher on the left.

Turn of the Century Burial Practices

They knew exactly how to phrase things after a lifetime of living
by their wits. It was as if their behavior demanded an explanation which,
had it not been oblique and emblematic, would have certainly
invited excessive interpretation, even reprisals. Intense and repeated
study of their language was to be our, their children's
central preoccupation nonetheless, creating, then impacting
our perceptions. Rituals and literary order were our fate
in this overarching universe – a structure unrelated to well-being.
They were soon to be invisible, a product of our intellect,
and inessential from the religious point of view. It is no wonder
that such figures have acquired a disaffected air, being wholly
anachronistic and supernatural.

Something You Can Do with Your Clothes On

When he went out to lunch one day in 2009,
he could not have imagined that he would
simply cease to exist. There's no hard and fast rule
about existence as long as you recognize seminal events
along the way, which may help you sense
when a new idea is about to surface.

Sprawling on a Pin

Never underestimate the power of surprise. That reasonable woman will ask you about the city of your birth, which languages you spoke there and how the tenor of your present life compares to your recollections. She may also ask you about your sexual preferences, in the plural, though she's wondering silently whether you prefer dogs over cats. Despite what you think, these are all serious, emotionally authentic matters. Do not be trapped, however, by that old assumption: the question you most dread may not be asked, and your responses might lead her to cast your story in a more sympathetic, less violent or coercive light. It will be worth your while to answer her sincerely – this sounds complex, but is really very simple. Although you may quote Derrida, for example, on the true meaning of first language, it may serve just as well and be great fun to quote your mother, thereby demonstrating tolerance and love. Foucault is best not mentioned, but will stand you in good stead. If she asks about recycling, make your answer as well-meaning as an empty plastic bin.

Touch Typing Contracts Forever

I can't get through the days
typing as my Dad would say
without you.
Nights on my lumpy hard futon
are not bad for my back.
During the day, I work at
something that is not far
from a good and relevant
piece of work, but without
you it falls flat repeatedly
I might as well be touch
typing contracts without
a break forever.
Retrograde Lament
Lamenting
can't get through the days
only typing
without you although lamentably lumpy
hard futon nights are not bad for the back.
During the day
working at something
not far from
a good and relevant work opportunity
falls flat repeatedly without you.
Might as well be touch typing contracts
lamenting without a break forever.
Forever
Touch typing and lamenting
can't get through the days
hard futon night
working at something
good, relevant, flat without
lamenting without typing
contracts

My Beautiful Ballooning Heart

post-trauma poems

APICAL BALLOONING (aka Takotsubo Cardiomyopathy & Broken Heart Syndrome):

"Transient apical ballooning (also known as Takotsubo cardiomyopathy) is a syndrome characterized by apical left ventricular dysfunction that mimics myocardial infarction, often in the absence of significant coronary artery disease. It is an important consideration in patients with acute chest pain, since the signs and symptoms are identical to those of an ACS. The syndrome typically occurs in patients following a severe emotional stress. ... For patients who survive the acute episode, the disorder is usually self-limited. Left ventricular function typically recovers within 1-4 weeks."   [Jason Ryan and Eli V. Gelfand, Chapter 5: Special considerations in acute coronary syndromes: Acute transient apical ballooning syndrome, pp.133-134 in Management of Acute Coronary Syndromes, Eli Gelfand and Christopher Cannon, John Wiley & Sons Ltd. 2009.]

"Transient left ventricular apical ballooning, also known as takotsubo cardiomyopathy, is an unusual abnormality that may be the underlying cause of signs and symptoms of acute myocardial infarction (AMI) in a small number of patients. ... This abrupt onset of extensive "ballooning" or dilatation of the left ventricle occurs most often in postmenopausal women after a traumatic psychosocial or physical stressor. ... Apical ballooning was first described in the Japanese literature in the early 1990s.... The original name given to apical ballooning was takotsubo cardiomyopathy, which was derived from the shape of the narrow-necked bulging "takotsubo" container used by Japanese fisherman to trap octopus. The shape of the takotsubo pot resembles the distorted ballooning ventricle."   [Transient left ventricular apical ballooning. McCulloch, Brenda, Critical Care Nurse, December 1, 2007.]

My Beautiful Ballooning Heart

for Ruti

I
The impact of a bully on the left half of the heart
is like a thief in the night who breaks in
through the bathroom window by beating
the bars with a stone repeatedly –
that one last blow that bends the bars
lets the brutal bandit steal, not your sheaves
of wheat to shift them to his own pile
of golden grain, but the true objects of his desire –
the tools of your livelihood and the ring,
all that's left of one you love.

II
The largest and most muscular chamber of my heart
will sail us away to the land we dreamed of –
we only need to attach the strings
and stand underneath
and let it rise.

III
Volatile spirit, take a deep breath
and contain yourself. Do not allow his cruelty
to cause you to break your own heart.

IV
When he asked to be referred to
by ordination only, it was a sign;
when he lorded over the air-conditioning,
it was a sign; when he raised the cost
of your insurance to reduce the cost
of his, it was a sign; when he preached
withholding ice cream from his tiny daughter
proudly and demanded blind obedience and threatened

repercussions, evaluation, termination,
when he clarified to you that he was either in or he was
out.

V
Heed the signs of your spirit created
in your left ventricle. Do not be frightened
by the pain
s
in your chest
the lightning bolts before your eyes. Act
judiciously, spill your guts to those in
authority and walk away while your heart
still beats reasonably well in that chest
to the emergency room where they will
misdiagnose you almost kill you if you
haven't already died and then save you –
both from them and from yourself, but not from him.

VI
A shock to your system, post traumatic stress,
and maybe acid reflux just for muddying the waters
of recovery. You are fine but will you tolerate
a stress test just to be sure?

VII
The rest of the stressors do not go away.
Let's send them on a vacation to Bolivia.
Let's put them on a train.
Up up and away
high above my beautiful ballooning heart.

VIII
I am broken
and should be returning to the family farm
the old boys are still there and have become
doctors by now. They've missed me. We can

lie on a tarp on the grass surrounded by the
potted plants they brought me when they
looked at my face and knew that not only
am I older, I have not been well. A public
park will do if the family has no farm. I'll
strap on my pedometer and do a few laps,
weigh myself on my new digital scale
and take my own blood pressure now and
again between kisses.

IX
The impact of a bully upon the younger generation
is not limited to tabloids and TV. Tragedy easily descends
down our offender's bony fingers down down to
curse our children, forced to gather round
leaving
their unguarded households prey
to local predators who are essentially the same
as our white collar tough. A curse upon his head.

X
The impact of a bully
can be measured in words, lines, stanzas
that will not fly. Deflated left ventricles
hurrah

XI
Assessment oriented
continued impact
variables
and unknown
and his life goes on.

Comfort Out

I came back to one of the hotels I used to stay in
before they changed from comfort to holiday.
The derelicts were camped on the driveway
to the left of the entrance, and I walked by them
on my way in –
bunkered next to their tall piles of charcoal stones
and concrete blocks, more permanent fixtures even
than the wandering stray figure
that used to weave in and out
of the lobby in the comfort days.

Just to Watch It Burn

Shut up! Prepare for assault, my dear.
Help is on the way. You'll be okay.
Go ahead, my dear, let it out.
State the nature of the problem,
talk to me! It's a start. We're
in trouble, and everything else
is just talk. There. I said it.

I am at a loss, but my memory
will keep going and going.
I am at a loss, and you
are hiding. Let me get this straight –
you are a little bit sensitive and comfortable
within your boundaries. Not so close!

Oh, for Pete's sake, it's a trap.
You can only be
either a prisoner or a casualty
(your memory will live on).

We're all scared. Are you all right? You'll be okay.
Surrender and completely transform.
It's now or never to do what you can.
Resume. Remember, even your own
toughest judge gets angry about what happened.

Keep Watch

Keep watch
Although the roaring
And the hissing
And the humming
Of the traffic in the
rain and a
closing door
Across the hall and
Clicking heels from
The ceiling cause
You to close your eyes.

I Will Show You

On a beach in San Diego
Or hiding in Northampton

In your own back yard
Or in selected theaters only

Each party shall exchange
Their maps and party favors

with the other

Moving on should always be a
Celebration of the triumph of

one over the other

The beginning of a drive
To unidentified distractions

Undoing

It's so embarrassing
Every single survival photograph
Notwithstanding the hard work
and the transforming vision
of grandeur in the lens
is a concept that came cheap.
Cross-checking any sense
of moral outrage
takes the camera
out of hand, smears
the paint across
the canvas and
relegates images
to the realm of
the undone. Try
this. Remember
how it felt to hear
the beating of his voice.

Second Urban Legend

The man who coined the term
psychedelic welcomed migraines
as harbingers of the divine until
zigzag bolts of colored lightning
first floated across his sight,
more evil than sawteeth,
ice bright and beyond his control.

Quaver

If I cannot see or smell
Or touch you either,
Perhaps I can hear you –
My quaver.
I have known quavers
that touched me
from thousands of
miles away. It is
the sense of your
sensing the same
as I sense
Our lifting the pen
striking the keys
in tandem
or face to face
responding
to a self-same
disembodied pulse.

No It's Not

It is a new land
strange paradise
institutional headquarters
the Amazon
a book
storage
a whole bunch
myriads
confusing
in every language.
Keep it away.
Say, Joe, it
pulses in my jugular.
Guard the door!

Say Joe

guard the door please
two transparent plastic chairs
a black centimeter ruler
Pink Pearl Eraser
package of twelve colored pencils

Capturing Contour Lines

What indication of steepness did you have
when, virtually undamaged, you were
busy drawing maps
with trusted friends
who'd never been to the mine?

crystals
tiny decomposed
labeled simply *Human*
with their thick golden sawtooth blades
their virtually undamaged
narrow white pyramid faces
razor thin

By tying together two rubber bands
you now compare their charts to yours,
anchoring your pencil securely
without covering more than necessary,
making and testing predictions
about how figures alter
when you move.

Keep focused to find what works best
It's not necessary to stress
There is magic in the rubber to help you
capture contour lines.

What governs their shapes and patterns?
What indications of steepness they give!
Though you'll need to take note of
closeness, lack of distance and the appearance of depth,
they'll prepare you to negotiate as steep a slope as possible.

From the Heap

I
Who can get to the bottom of our error?
If success tends to lie in simplicity,
then we're doomed to decompose
without delay. To avoid decomposition,
we'd need such a large collection
of observations and comparisons comparisons.
Inherent in the defect of our present method
are endless attempts at dispassionate expression.

II
"Your prediction of events elicited a
feeling approaching awe and pointed
to certain errors into which all
are liable to fall
when swayed
to give it all away.
You showed once again that
remarkable exceptions to general rules
are not peculiar to living beings."

Turn to the Nucleus, the Eye

Turn to the nucleus, the eye, and limit
sentiment. What was concealed in him
stacked up pitiless. Posing him
jubilant, holding a bunch of daisies
with a monarch butterfly circling his head,
makes the picture no less terrifying.

I Have a Tolerance

Exploration
of self-absorption
in preparation
for practices different from yours
or the same.
If I suddenly cried, "All hands on deck!"
on the slope of a deserted Las Ramblas
at night
would you comply even though
there was a very slight
reason for you to fear?
Let's say you were
immersed in discussion,
not absorbed in joy,
and would be denied
me
at times in the future.
Who was it who decided
for the best
despite our differences and
while my humanity made way for hate?
I have a tolerance for self-absorbed types, I mean
I respect
my condescending attitude,
presume they are inferior.

How It Has Always Worked

To begin with, he was standing in front of me at first,
taking it all in. He was my holy grail just
for the taking and fell to his knees just
to grant me a feeling of height. "Just
this," he said, "and no more." Then,
he rose again to his full stature just
before circling slowly until he stood
directly behind me. It was only then
and not before, regardless of what
others may tell you,
that I fell to my knees to avoid
asymmetry, which can be so
damaging to any relationship.

Not a Navy Wife

I am not a navy wife
and not on active duty
not a coward or a fool
gestures to the gallery
Following a twenty-three year deployment
to the Mediterranean Sea,
I returned to my station by the waters,
thriving in captivity. A discovery team
unearthed me and advised me
enthusiastically of my rights.
Like a plaster cast of my living face,
my countenance smiled on them:
I am not a navy wife
and not on active duty
not a coward or a fool
gestures to the gallery

So Relieved

hukal li I was so relieved. In the Holy Tongue,
it sounds elegant for some reason. Why not? I had used
the form before
and had a strong desire for some reason
to translate its tight, slightly retro,
understatedly tart message in today's lingo and to use it
perhaps slightly
sarcastically for some reason on this side of the moon, too.
Here in the semi-darkness of my native tongue,
I had reason to wish to say
perhaps tongue in cheek,
"I'm SO relieved."

Uncontrollable

The uncontrollable mystery on the bestial floor.
from *The Magi*, W.B. Yeats

I looked at you and thought you were a statue
and saw my world as empty. Such a waste,
that uncontrollable mystery on my parquet floor.
When you came to life again, transformed by my gaze
From papier-mâché into the man you were,
We transcribed you in the book of life. In the blink of an eye,
I ripped out the page, pleated you into a fan, cooled myself down,
Crumpled the fan into a ball, tossed it in the air and caught it.

Crossing with the Light

Instead of me, why not love others, I said
as we crossed the tracks on our way to the 7-11
at twilight. Japanese Taiko drumbeats
from the dance studio devoured you
and an inbound street car
turned my words to ash. This was a lucky break,
I thought, since that was not what I meant to say
at all. I'd been walking up Beacon to Harvard
when you'd turned to me in my mind
and told me that we'd stay together
to an overripe old age,
fat and unaesthetic and totally
into each other. On the corner of Summit,
the walk light was recommending that I wait.

The Hand of God

From the back it looks like
the great wall of China,
which I have never seen.

Demise

We'd be remiss if we did not note
genitalia and mourn the demise
of the era's greats.

Infinitely in Every Direction

What if the
last time I saw you was

through a rectangular structure
of toothpicks and straight-edged corks?

Was I
second, third or fourth?

When we meet again,
will there be a change for the better?

A triangle or a straight line?

The bread bears were aligned
in a square basket.

Go Ahead

Go ahead
Be angry
when I lose
your edge
All your edges
This is my entry
for February 20th
in which I can
still discern your
shape although
you are present
only by inference
No photo below
explains
your transition
into white

Left to Its Own Devices

my heart races.
Two color photos of a high school girl
from the 1960's were slipped
into the pages of a book
in the 1980's that found its place
in an extensive personal library that
may no longer exist. The Taiko drums
across the street
slow my pulse
then raise it up.
How many beats per minute
did the doctor say?
How many beats per line?

Rehovot and Jerusalem, Jerusalem and Rehovot

How well do you recall just moving
into a new suite of offices that your employer
called "too Arab" because of the pale
turquoise walls and green door trim?
Did his remark propel you back to the
green ironwork you had ordered for the
windows of your new apartment
ten years earlier? Every ten years,
you might conclude, there comes
a moment of great
embarrassment when viewed
through another's eyes.
Not to trivialize, but the other
construction-related problem
that comes to mind from those days,
for both those decades,
has to do with the placement of
light switches. In the first, they were
placed outside the bedroom doors.
In the second, the master switch that
thrust you into total darkness
when you worked alone late
into the night
was located several steps
from the exit door.

They Dance

Is this the unanticipated
so romantic kiss behind the curtain

before it goes up when the overture concludes
or after it comes down at the end of Act I

of the final dress rehearsal the day before the show,
before our soft-shoe, right after our duet?

In either case,

eternally dressed in my powder-blue gown,
now at last I know that this kiss leads on cue,
just in time, to a powerful slap across the face

by a not so innocent third party who brings me
back to earth before she vanishes upstage

and we two once again take center stage
and dance.

Why He Took It

       To be fair, I should tell you up front that he may not have taken it at all. I may have taken it or almost anybody else intentionally to put it to some momentary use and then absent-mindedly not replaced it or with the judicious thought of putting it (i.e., me) out of harm's way at least for the time being.

Miraculously Relaxed

If your therapist
were your fairy godmother,
magic and miracles
would flow from her wand
causing far less disturbance
passing through the air
than this Bombardier Q400
turboprop, purportedly "quiet
inside and out.... (The 'Q'
stands for quiet)." Its seventy
seats are almost all full
this evening. The cabin noise
and vibration suppression (NVS) system
doesn't seem to be doing much good,
and the sneezing a seat or two up
continues. Still, I can confirm, giggling
quietly while I read the inflight magazine,
that their claim of "lowest fuel burn
per seat" is accurate enough. I rewrap half
of the turkey & cheddar on whole wheat
with seeds, all that the terminal Starbucks
had, and return it to the mini brown
paper shopping bag propped
in the corner of my tray table against
the wall and the back of 6D. I am
wedged in here, fifty pounds
overweight (well, twenty-five) though
I'd swear my original reservation was
for an aisle seat, always an aisle seat.
Wedged in here, I might like to know
the disposition of the world waiting
to receive me below. I'd like to
predict which movie my date will
recommend and whether our
prime minister will persist
in whipping the masses into a frenzy,
prepping the silver platter
to serve up another course. The scent

of cold cuts insinuates itself
through layers of brown paper
and reclosed plastic wrap. It is good
that the tall thin suit next to me picks
veggie chips off the cart
packed in their yellow-orange bag
that propels a pungent ripple through the air
when he pops it open. Food not shared,
bread not broken, love unrequited
on some lush terrain back on earth.
Whether the original author chose
to tell the tale of food
from the point of view of those
who control our resources or
to tell the tale of politicians
by means of the food they eat
in silence, literally avoiding
rubbing elbows for an hour
and a half between here and there,
the price of a ticket – movie, plane or
love, will take a fully-ripened
lifetime to earn and will be
appraised in light of whether
or not I wake up a day or so later
alone at 4 a.m. and decide against
turning the hotel alarm clock
one hour forward. Next,
a text message will arrive canceling
the remainder of our plans. Long after
we are gone, proliferation will continue,
at least for a number of years. When
will there ever again be two Hebrew-
speaking Ashkenazi Jews, a man
and a woman on a Saturday afternoon
in North America, holding hands,
miraculously relaxed,
viewing a Japanese film with not
a bag of popcorn between them?

Misdoings of This or That Life

While half the people forget for years at a time, a quarter
will narrate in detail the misdoings of a past life,
more readily than their misdeeds of late,
anticipating that your response will be limited to
a gentle sort of astonishment, more curious than judgmental.

While simultaneous lives thrill us with their overlappings,
crisscrossings, cut corners, near-collisions and clenched fists,
past lives serve up your basic bread and butter sandwiches, but
thicker than you can get your mouth around without the filling
plopping out onto the floor to be overlooked hopefully forever.

Approximately one quarter of everyone on the planet
is preoccupied with trying to remember what they know they
must have done in a past life. I'm so busy with present misdoings
that I sometimes forget for years at a time what I did.

Getting a Raise

I was a soap opera heroine
the good

white witch

ingenuous and well-meaning
mainly. I was caught up

in a chronic condition
of stepping forward
over the abyss.

Their names were

mainly interchangeable.

Mine were as predictable
as bought pies. Feeling the pain

stirring soup on camera picking up
something at the deli on her way
home witch. The pay was less than

the black witch's.

Watching,
Strictly for Entertainment Purposes

Tame girls, sometimes called dancing girls, are wild girls that were captured when young or born and bred in captivity. While their use is most likely frowned upon in your circles, girls still perform as tourist attractions around the world. Their use as street entertainment, however, is generally criticized. What a reminder that geographically, for all eternity, self-sacrifice is distorted and misconstrued and makes little sense. What shakes me up behind the scenes is that there is an element of self-sacrifice in every relationship – in almost every act. Unbelievable! It's up to you to improve your quality of life by giving more, even when you are completely submerged in an ocean of love.

Huge Buddha Doodle

I wish I had asked them to get me

Ferlinghetti's signature. Zvi did

When he visited City Lights

And bought a book.

Maybe LF was just down the

Street sipping a decaf java.

I treasure the doodle

By AG given to me by

NY. AG not only signed

His collected poems for

NY, he encircled the

Entire frontispiece with a

Huge Buddha doodle.

Food for thought

When next I hesitate

To sign my books at all.

Automotive

It feels so natural to us –
keeping it all under control.
Men especially, but not exclusively,
have been said to feel more like
their natural selves looking
in the rear-view.
Not the mirroring of the self that is
falling in love again – not that stage,
which disrupts routines.
Better gas up in time this time
because the route is sober
and an automobile is just
that.

When Chaos Has Come and Gone

If all your fantasies
were eventually to
come true
the question would remain
whether you would retain
beneath the surface
the savagery of
an earlier life
when citizens conjoined
for a day for an hour
for a lifetime for a weekend
and stayed authentic
though artfully nonchalant
constantly concerned
though genuinely passionate
giving all yet contemplating
the wholly unknown life abroad
or at home of their other halves,
thirds, quarters, fifths, etc. For all
our dignity and attempts at calm
we are by nature turbulent
and, what's more, ignorant
of the devices of nobility.

the week before we meet is

the week before we meet is
like a prizefight every time or a
marathon uphill through brambles
over rocks even quicksand every
road sign brings tears to my eyes
there are moats around every
neighborhood that turn into
rushing rivers of tragic proportions
that sweep innocent commuters
to their deaths the week before
we meet the week before we
meet stands all my competitors
the entire team in their striped
jerseys up straight and linked
into an impenetrable wall
guarding against my carefree
kick that blasts the ball on goal

Taking the Weight off Your Shoulders

Looking the other way involves
the unabridged English language.
Taking the weight off your shoulders
is a simpler affair.
Knowing you need to be somewhere
walking in off the street
hearing them speak knowing
you're among your own and
being happy.

Catching the Mouse

Out of the corner of my eye
I caught the mouse
who slipped under my front door
who made a dash
for the coat closet
at 6 a.m.
Was I at last ready
to explore the possibility that I
could become my own counterpart?
"A figure with a home
inviting those in need of wisdom
to enter" as M.D. Coogan once put it?
"Come, eat of my bread"
and of my winter coat and "walk
in the way of insight."
Shall I become
orderly and successful
the proverbial personification
of a good catch?
My speech will be no longer foolish
and seductive –
strange?

How to Ask for What You Want

How about a bowl of soup
Could it be that simple, this
sacramental moment
rings
an offering
rain of fire
not by accident
fundamental
Ask
And you may receive

Current Events and a Chorus

there should have been
visible to my naked eye
a total eclipse of the moon
on Tuesday at midnight
but an electrical storm
came between us
there should have been
visible from the British Isles
a total eclipse of the sun
on August 28 1184 BC
but that is all I know and
perhaps
all I shall never know

imprinted with the seal of the West
is a tradition with a past but no future
passionate full of turmoil and conflicts
having all this aesthetic distance yet
not lacking the ethos of the warrior or
the bathos of the victim of independence

it has taken me by storm
a polished tradition more startling
than any heretofore unexplored
unresolved internal romantic struggle

than the unresolvable struggles
of the eternally romantic
unresolvable is fine
irresolvable sounds awkwardly
American

imprinted with the seal of the West
is a tradition with a past but no future
passionate full of turmoil and conflicts
having all this aesthetic distance yet
not lacking the ethos of the warrior or
the bathos of this victim of independence

Double Portion

I meet a tall imposing figure
dressed in red
known in the field
(we have met once before
under awkward circumstances
as I munched the double portion
she'd been compelled to abandon)
everybody knows her
her opinion must have weight
we exchange a cheery hello
after eying one another twice
across the conference hall

Way back in the beginning
in a college dining commons
I met an unimpressive girl
whom it seemed I had supplanted
(I'd seen her once before
as she exited his off campus rooms
with an armful of books
just as I arrived)
she warned me now
that I would suffer
down the line
as she had suffered
or did she merely eye me briefly
from across the dining commons
chuckling to her new boyfriend
before she took a seat
and ate her lunch

Without Benefit of Job

Like Satan going to and fro
and up and down on earth,
his latter years
are testing him unfairly.

Is he to believe
that no sins
or tragic flaws
spelling mistakes
missed appointments
vacant stares
manifold past
or present
romantic wrong-
or right-
doings
account for his agony?

Without benefit of Job
he is high priest
driven by grief to God
with flames ignited in his gut
combusting his own well-being.

A Sort of Proposal

A few years ago
there might have been other options.
It hit me right in the stomach
at that moment.
I hadn't yet decided –
I had to think about it over time.
If he'd given me just a minute more...
Normally, I was the perfect person
for this kind of reflection
on the spot
but I'd been working
around the clock of late.
I'm still considering my options.
What are the pros and cons?
We all take such matters
much too seriously.

emptying her place
of stacks of hallmark roses
a red wheel barrow

How I Can Tell I'm Not Depressed

When Rabbi Dr. A. Twerski says,
describing a certain kind of
depression, "…when a person
looks at a blackboard
and thinks it's a window
and sees the world as hopeless,"
he (Rabbi Dr. Twerski) is
not depressed, I'm thinking, since
he is hoping we are listening,
looking (me) at the laptop screen
and thinking it's a window.

After This Mysterious Moment with You

Even after this mysterious
Effusive
Everlasting moment
here
with you
when I
Cast off this or that convention
Exalt sporadic gestures of my brain
I remain the daughter of my parents
wife of my husbands
friend of my lovers
friend of my friends

On Gunmetal Gray Sheets

Rose was making love with Arik Einstein
Who all along was you
Though you were in pain
548 miles away
Rose was
Kissed

Words Can Be Obstacles

Black ice counteracts my quest to get to the other shore
Intercepts my tenuous footfalls
Interjects a note that is tremulous
I hesitate before applying my soles to
What appears to be pavement
Ten steps from the embankment

As Expected Brunch in the Afterglow

You could develop a habit
of staring at people
you have never
encountered before, disguise yourself
as a stranger, wear
orange reading glasses
and excessively gelled hair.
You could not give a damn
about a handsome stranger
who takes the table
behind you, a moving form
in your periphery, or
turn around and stare directly into his eyes,
which would not be as blue as your lover's
across town in a meeting.

ROSE AROSE

1) Gunmetal Gray Sheets

Rose was making love with Arik Einstein
an Israeli crooner from the 60's
who all along was another man
who was in pain that night
548 miles away.
Rose was kissed.

2) Brunch in the Afterglow

Rose could develop a habit
of staring at people
she has never
encountered before, disguise herself
as a stranger, wear
orange reading glasses
and excessively gelled hair.
Rose could not give a damn
about a handsome stranger
who takes the table behind her,
a moving form in her periphery,
or she could turn around and stare
directly into his eyes,
which would not
be as blue as her lover's
across the city in a meeting.

3) Rose Arose

Fresher sheets than the last one
thought Rose
Twice the space
Half the price
sang Rose
but the bathroom switch

had been difficult to find
and the dinner menu
was missing dessert.
There would be
better breakfast food.
Rose arose and decided he
must be God.

4)   There Is Nothing Compelling About Rose

She is deniable. Rose is
controvertible. Rose cannot
imagine just how questionable
she is. She is rhetorically
an ineffective argument
why or why not
why not
why
critiqued in the margin   here.
Imagine you are having
a conversation with Rose.
Would you have a conversation
with Rose?

5)   In Other Societies

In other societies, reasons Rose.
In other ages, reasons Rose.
In other families, reasons Rose.

6)   Rose Is Thinking

about war religion politics food
controversy
spiritualism
studying
teaching
and popular science.
There are cigarette butts

at the foot of the stoop
to the left of the entrance
where she waits for Pierre
and his blue and white taxi.
Pierre's girlfriend of seven years
can spend an hour and a half
doing her hair and then takes it all
out and starts again. She's on the
frontlines at a luxury hotel
and must look right. Rose is
thinking about cutting her hair
when Pierre pulls up.

7)   On the Open Market

Not quite equal
to the situation

exchanging goods and services
one for another

one with the other
not open after all

not equal after all,
Rose signed her non-compete

clause long ago.
Not quite equal to the challenge

of social issues and troubled
visions

of animal might
exercising its muscles

trivializing Roses.

8) Equanimous

Rose walks the walk.
She is Woman Equanimous
despite her diffident innards.
She draws conclusions
from facts that can only be suggested
in the wake of various public scandals.
In her heart of hearts she predicts
that she will solve the problem.
She calls herself to action
to think ahead
to make nothing inadvertent
to not get caught.
Nighttime does not represent
a major setback or an obstacle.
It reminds the dreamer of
who she is.

Walking on a Cloud of Defense

With radio glee
reporting live
from the 108th
Santa Claus Parade,
I shuttled
to my last connection
on the fifth day
a fish and fowl day,
over the sea into the air day,
like creation.
The night before,
I'd left the Land
despite a defensive delay
on the Tel Aviv runway.
It was on this fifth day
that I counted
Jezreel clouds
still in pillars
before my eyes
near Pearson Airport
where I rested
at the Holiday Inn
with my iPhone
on my pillow.
Ahmad Tibi
and Ron Dani'el –
neither fish nor fowl
on Canadian soil –
indulged themselves
on my hand-held screen
above the "day five" caption
shouting about the children.
Who cares more

about the children?

By the time I was back

In Boston roasting

A turkey

It seemed that the

Ceasefire would hold.

The Creation of Today

after the inexplicable
disappearance and much later
return of the primordial house
painter

the just can't do refrain
the not here but there vision
lie still let it happen creation
a rotary in Rehovot Israel
at the bathroom sink
in North America
could be just such a there

an Italian poet
waiting for her in Italy
in a sunrise dream of mine
is what is sad
about our lives

can't do this
on the elevator
can't do this
peering over the wooden fence
at the dumpster
sixty years ago
where a no longer plush
monkey was tossed
into that box

not moving from the couch
lying on the beach
collecting flies

One Language One Speech

Everyone wants to write a
midrash
Or so the saying goes
Everyone wants to think
A midrash
As they're walking down the
street
Waiting for the light at Beacon
and Marion
Everybody wants to live a
Midrash
To get the punchline and the
nuances
To understand the vocab and the
sentence structures.
Everybody wants to share a
Midrash with their old, not too
intimate friends.
It's the third word that turns the
key.
Did you hear the one about
Genesis eleven?

Our Love Is Clean

Our love is clean.
The space between us
is Rodeo Drive
pumping altered ambergris
and cedar out to passersby.
Unlike the trash tracks
broadcast from entryways
on Yonge Street, we are sea that
sprays on Atlantic Ave. in April
and unejaculated jasmine
daydreams on Herzl.

The Stewardess Is Wearing a Pale Lipgloss

My ex-mother-in-law
god rest her soul
loved a true red lipstick.
My colleague's husband cannot
stand her bombshell pink.
I left my lavender luster
and its sugarberry twin behind
in my other purse
and had to buy a chapstick
at the terminal kiosk
and add a touch
of cream blush in the hope
that it won't make my lips
look too dull
or too fleshy
for my lover's taste
when I land over the border
and meet him
at the baggage carousel.

Archetypes, Harpies and Other Obstructions

When I cry out at night
shout
it is not about you
but about my workaday
interplay
inability
to satisfy the anima
made manifest
in this or that sister.

Supine

Young David was set upright
but I laid him down.

I stroked his left, still blameless
shoulder,
biceps,
hip

and marble upper thigh again
and again and again and again,

then put him back on his feet
in the manner of il Divino

after the ancient Greeks.

Remove My Obsession Mosaic

reMove my Obsession with Stunning
Attempts to Implement Completion
my Overnight Schemes And
Ideas about Checkered Moons
and Suns And Inspirations of others
Calling to Me Obsessively
And Incessantly Calling to
Me and calling to me to Objectify in Simple
Icons of Checkerboard Mosaic
when OutSide there Are animals in dreams
like three-legged Cats in a Meadowfull Of
Sunlight Aroused by my Incantations

eMulating Overjoyed Sliding on their backs
After Intolerable Control

Alternative Drama

Filmmakers know how to
either grey down
the kitchen counter the cabinets
the utensils the pepper tin or

buff up the shine of a faucet
to intensify horror.
Parchment lampshades deaden
while bodies in a closet sport

knitted caps, and we
are careful to hook the chain
and throw the latch even when
the actor resembles Gary

Bissonnette. Do you remember
me, Gary? This afternoon, the
gleam of a lock in a Canadian
film spared us from death.

Animate

The breeze between the drapes
plumps the pillows smooths the cases
in this animated scene.
Lumbering past the hedges
he is reluctant to form a dream of upheaval.
It is a wound that looms violet
extending from the edge of the lawn
affixing itself to my windowsill
stitching the drapes all the way up.

Vault

There are two keys
to the vault
where her ring
hides out of reach.
Patience. You'll be
tracking in the snow
and tracking in
the sand
turning her
tangerine silk beads
over and over
on the cotton batting.
Her diabetes
became brittle.
Stay the flow.
Pencils sharpened
she'd capture the
light in your eyes
then erase it.

Knockout

This is a hidden metaphor
for heavyweight, as well as
for diction with gloves on.
Here, Marvelous Marvin
explodes and punctuates.
There, dutifully measured
anonymous jabs staccato
on vellum. "Nowhere
are you safe!" "I will pummel
you into submission."
Envisioning something
of the sort, you enter
the ring swinging.

AFTERWORD

Kissing

for Jacques Derrida

Joyously with great freedom deep
in my mouth my temporary language
of choice coats my cheeks my throat
tongue teeth lips inner inside and here
on this page

You are dragging me back second language
first language
of mine
language of a kiss on the lips by a second
lover soft lips and
tongue
language of
less discord
before my eyes longing to lick
your eyes

There are always two
he said
even when one is forgotten

Gedera 1999

Janice Silverman Rebibo, a Massachusetts native and native English speaker, is the author of four previous books of original poetry written primarily in Hebrew and a volume of popular Israeli poetry translated to English. Critics have called Rebibo's work a bold blend of two imposing literary traditions and a strategic breakthrough that added something new to the war of independence of Israel's consciousness. For over two decades, her Hebrew poetry was published and reviewed widely in Israel's major newspapers and literary journals. Her English poetry is currently accessible in a number of print anthologies and online journals originating in Israel and the United States.

For her fourth poetry collection, *Zara Betzion* [A Stranger-woman in Zion], Gvanim Tel Aviv, Rebibo received a President of Israel Award and the Israel Lottery Commission's Cultural Award, as well as the Steiner Prize from Hebrew College. *Within the Song To Live*, translations of poet Natan Yonatan, is now in its third printing, Gefen Jerusalem/New York.

Rebibo's poem "My Beautiful Ballooning Heart" was nominated by *Muddy River Poetry Review* for a 2012 Pushcart Prize. She is the *Soul-Lit* featured poet for summer 2013.

She was the 2013 judge of the RAVSAK North American Hebrew Poetry Contest for grades 1-12 and has translated and edited children's books as well as a broad range of scholarly texts – from literature, linguistics and education to medicine and hi-tech entrepreneurship. Rebibo calls both Brookline, Massachusetts, and Rehovot, Israel, home and has written and collaborated on pop lyrics and classical libretti for works produced in Boston, Tel Aviv and Moscow, and at Carnegie Hall. She has always welcomed the challenge of leading poetry writing workshops, most recently at Middlebury College, Vermont, at Brandeis University and in her local communities.

Rebibo holds BAJS and MAJS degrees with concentrations in Hebrew language and literature from Hebrew College. Her expanded thesis on biblical intertextuality, "Why Quote God? Three Modern Israeli Poets Allude to Sacred Texts," will be available in print in 2014. Since 1989, she has worked with non-profits dedicated to the revitalization of the Hebrew language and to the promotion of tolerance and cooperation among disparate sectors of Israeli society.

Poetry updates may be found on www.janicerebibo.com.